MW01282880

SUPERMAN TENNIS SERVE

Learn how to serve fastest serve ever with scientifically proven techniques!

By

Joseph Correa

COPYRIGHT

ACKNOWLEDGMENTS

This book is dedicated to my family for always being there no matter what the situation.

SUPPLEMENT

This book includes a supplemental training course which can be found by going to www.coachcorrea.com. It will provide you with additional tennis instruction and knowledge for you to take advantage of and improve your game. The only way to improve your game is by increasing your knowledge of the game.

INTRODUCTION

Superman Tennis Serve: Learn How To Serve Fastest Serve Ever With Scientifically Proven Techniques!

By Joseph Correa

Learn how to drastically change your serve through 6 exercises that will increase your racquet speed and acceleration in a very significant way.

This book includes: - The 6 Superman Tennis Serve exercises - The 3 charts that will teach you how to do them in an organized manner. - Detailed explanation on each phase of the charts. - 6 serving tips - 12 tennis competition tips to improve your overall game

This is your chance to have the best serve ever with this training that will change the way you approach your serve. Using a scientifically proven method to increase your racquet head speed and acceleration through 6 exercises. Do you want to start winning more matches thanks to your serve? Want to make a big difference in the results you have in your matches and tournaments? Well, in tennis, YOU SPEND AT LEAST 46% OF THE TIME SERVING! Which means that the better you serve, the better your chance is of controlling that 46% of your match. The remainder of the match you spend on returning serve and hitting ground strokes and volleys during the point. This basically means that working on your forehand, backhand, overhead, slice, topspin, return of serve, and other specific shots will account require a lot more time and effort to master the remaining 54% of your match. SO WHY NOT WORK ON WHAT MATTERS THE MOST?

This book will: - change how you serve. - It will reduce shoulder injuries. - It will reduce the amount of running you will have to do in your matches. - It will teach you how to serve faster than ever before - It will save you tears, frustration, losses, and most importantly losses

It includes 3 charts that explain in detail when to train, how to train, how many times to train, and what to train. Each chart is specific for before competition, during competition, and during your off season which may be in the summer or during the winter time so that you can maximize results. Make the investment in your game to change how you play and WIN MORE TROPHIES!

This book will teach you how to serve 10-20 mph faster in a 3 month day by day program. The best serve training program in the market. Video includes a 3 month chart training program and a step by step manual. This book shows you how to do the exercises properly and the process you should follow in order to be successful with the program.

This book includes a supplemental training course which can be found by going to www.coachcorrea.com.

ABOUT THE AUTHOR

Hello, my name is Joseph Correa and I have been training and teaching tennis for over 15 years. I played professional tennis for years and am now a USPTR professional certified coach.

After years of competing and training with some of the best in the world I have learned that most people can be very successful in competition with the right mental, physical, and emotional training.

Proven scientific techniques, drills, and step by step phases must be performed to reach your peak and for that reason I have prepared the first group of training DVD's and books showing you how to reach your goals.

Through my work and teaching aids, I have helped hundreds of amateur and professional tennis player's advance with their physical, mental, and performance goals to achieve great results.

I teach you everything I know you will need to reach your goals and hope you will enjoy and share these lessons and ideas with loved ones. To learn more about the different lessons taught through my books and DVD's go to www.tennisvideostore.com. Many more books will be coming out this year with some advanced drills and techniques.

Best of luck,

Joseph

TABLE OF CONTENTS

SUPERMAN TENNIS SERVE

Learn how to serve fastest serve ever with scientifically proven techniques!

By

Joseph Correa

PART 1

HOW TO PERFORM THE SUPERMAN SERVE EXERCISES

This is a training workout that produces results and will get you serving 10 to 20 mph faster than you originally served before starting this program. Remember that there are a number of things that contribute towards having a harder serve. We will go over them one at a time. Remember to work the program so that the program works for you. In other words, follow the charts and the manual without skipping steps or days in the training calendar so that you see results.

WHAT YOU WILL NEED

First of all let´s go over what you will need:

You will need:

1 TENNIS RACQUET (PREFERABLY YOURS)

10 TENNIS BALLS (ANY TYPE)

1 BOUNCEABLE MEDICINE BALL

1 STRETCHABLE OR ELASTIC EXERCISE BAND

TENNIS ATTIRE (COMFORTABLE EXERCISE CLOTHES)

TENNIS COURT

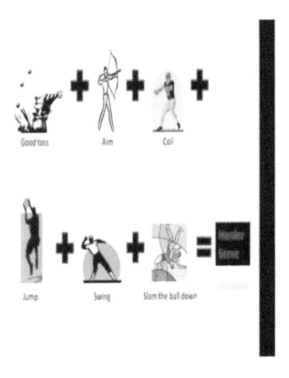

In order to serve harder you need to have 6 basic elements that work together as a team. In this case, we are going to focus on 6 exercises performed in different sports but used in a similar way as in the tennis serve.

Having a good toss just like a juggler is *the first* and most important element. Having a good toss equals having the potential of having a good serve and having a bad toss is the equivalent to never having a good serve. It only makes sense to think, that if you will be reaching a faster serving speed than your normal, you need to make sure the ball is at the right place at the moment of impact.

The second element is aim. If you want to have aim like an archer, proper posture is necessary. In tennis a proper posture is obtained by holding a "tennis trophy position" before starting your acceleration. Look for a tennis trophy and copy that position. You will see a similar form to an archer but directed upwards and with a deep knee bend.

The third element is coiling before hitting the ball. Most quarterbacks in football have incredible throwing power and the main reason why they can generate so much acceleration is because of their coiling position. Practice turning your shoulders more sideways so that you can turn towards the ball and use all of your upper body in a second (or as fast as you can, a fraction of a second would be ideal).

The fourth element is jumping. This is where most advanced tennis players get the additional speed on their serves. Basketball players are masters at creating a quick and powerful vertical leap. You should learn and apply this important factor to your serve to get the results you want even though it might take a while to learn to incorporate jumping and swinging together.

The fifth element is the swing acceleration. We use a baseball players throw to understand the fundamental technique behind a good throwing motion since it is very similar to a tennis players arm motion when swinging a tennis racquet and creating the necessary acceleration. By improving your throw, you will improve your swing. You will be working a lot on this in the training program so that you can throw further and further every time which will equate to a stronger serve.

The sixth and last element is to "slam the ball down". As important as it is to thrust your body upwards towards the ball, you still need the other half of the equation which is creating as much force downwards with both arms and upper body when impacting the ball while keeping your head up as to maintain eye contact.

These are the 6 serve training exercises you will be doing:

Tennis ball throw

Serve accelerations

Squat jumps

Medicine ball throws

Band triangle

Complete serves

Tennis ball throws should be done with a relaxed motion just like a baseball pitchers throw. Start with your weight on your back foot and finish with your weight on your right foot (for a righty, for a lefty it would be backwards). Try to make sure your elbow is bent as a straight arm throw will only injure your shoulder. Use your left arm to help you turn faster by turning it to the left as your throw. You will be implementing a similar left arm pull when you serve but it will be from a vertical angle downwards as you begin impact on the ball.

Serve accelerations are the backbone of these series of exercises so make sure to do them properly. Using serve accelerations as part of your pre-serve warm up is very effective and will reduce shoulder, elbow, and wrist injuries. Serve accelerations are service swings you perform without the use of a tennis ball, which means, you are actually swinging at the air and creating a swooshing sound when you start going faster. The friction between your racquet and the air creates this whistling sound. Prepare just like a normal serve, include your jump and follow through. Finish by stepping or landing in front of the baseline. Always finish in front of the baseline. NO JUMPING BACKWARDS! If you jump backwards you will never learn to use your body weight to increase serve velocity.

Squat jumps are very simple exercises that can be done on court but it's better if you do them on grass or a softer surface to minimize knee impact. Also, have comfortable shoes that will absorb as much of the impact as possible since you will be performing many jumps. Bend your knees with your legs apart and your hips and gluts downwards toward the ground without letting your knees go forward (just like sitting on a chair!). Going forward with your knees causes unnecessary strain on your knees and keeping your knees together will hurt joints and ligaments so stay away from these two things. Use your arms to propel you upwards as you jump into the air. When landing on the ground, bring your feet together to reduce impact every time you perform this exercise.

As you repeat the squat jumps every week you should be jumping higher off the ground and this will equate to a lot more momentum towards your arm. The additional strength in your legs will help not only improve your acceleration but also will give you a higher point of impact which will help you get more serves in.

Medicine ball throws need to be performed with a ball that is acceptable to your strength level. Do not use a medicine ball over 20 pounds as it will only make your serve slower instead of faster. Try different balls and see which one is comfortable for you. Choose one based on the amount of repetitions that you see in the training chart that you can complete with proper technique. Good form is everything. You want to strengthen the right muscles every time you exercise. You should start with the ball behind your head and elbows bent. Bend your knees and throw the ball straight down so that it bounces back up to your shoulder level. Catch the ball and repeat as many times as the chart requires.

Band triangle training is advanced and needs to be done properly to gain maximum results. Start by getting down on your right knee if you are right handed (and the opposite for left-handed players).

Next, place the band around a sturdy object such as a fence, tree, net post, or other. Take the band with your right hand and bend your elbow as to complete a pushing and pulling motion with your right arm just like you would when you do a serve. At the same time pull your left elbow down towards your left ribs as to feel them contract and then simply go back to the same starting position which should not have any resistance on your right or left hand, and then repeat as required by the training chart. Find a band that is right for you.

A Complete Serve requires you to perform as many serves as stated by the training chart. Try to push and pull with all the muscles you previously worked out in the last 5 exercises of the training program. In other words you want to make sure you are jumping, coiling, accelerating, swinging, and pulling down towards the ball on every serve. Your objective should be to work all the pieces of your serve separately and then on the 6th exercise bring them all together as a stronger and faster serve.

All 6 exercises need to be performed in the same order and with as many repetitions as required in the work out charts. Do not alter or change the order, amount, technique, or position in which you are supposed to complete them as it might change the results negatively.

PART 2

INTERPRETING THE CHARTS

Go over each chart and determine two things:

What stage of training are you in? <u>Competition stage</u> is when you are in the middle of competition. <u>Pre-competition</u> is when you are a few months away from competing. <u>Off season</u> is the third stage and this is when you are not competing nor in pre-competition. Each chart is for a specific stage of competition so make sure you decide where you are at since the difficulty level of each chart changes drastically.

What level tennis player are you? Beginner, Intermediate, and Advanced. Each level will affect the difficulty and repetitions for each exercise. If you find one level to be too difficult you can always move down a level and move up as your ability and strength improves.

Once you have these two things clear go to the chart and columns on the chart that best describes where you are at so that you may begin training.

ALWAYS WARM UP BEFORE STARTING THE SUPERMAN TENNIS SERVE EXERCISES!

THE SUPERMAN SERVE TRAINING CHARTS

SERVE HARDER TRAINING WORKOUT SCHEDULE

Workout Training Chart

Pre-Competition

MONTH 1

MONTH 2

MONTH 3

3 SERIES EACH

YOU SHOULD BE SERVING AT LEAST 10 MPH FASTER IF YOU WANT TO REACH PAST 10 MPH COMPLETE MONTH 3

YOU WILL BE SERVING HARDER THAN EVER BEFORE! MAKE SURE TO WARM UP BEFORE AND STRETCH AFTER TRAINING TO PREVENT INJURIES.

CONGRATS YOU SHOULD BE PAST 20 MPH FROM YOUR ORIGINAL SERVICE SPEED

Workout training Chart

During Off Season

YOU SHOULD BE SERVING AT LEAST 10 MPH FASTER. IF YOU WANT TO REACH PAST 10 MPH COMPLETE MONTH 3.

YOU WILL BE SERVING HARDER THAN EVER BEFORE! MAKE SURE TO WARM UP BEFORE AND STRETCH AFTER TRAINING TO PREVENT INJURIES.

CONGRATS YOU SHOULD BE SERVING PAST 20 MPH FROM YOUR ORIGINAL SERVICE SPEED.

YOU SHOULD BE SERVING ATLEAST 10 MPH FASTER IF YOU WANT TO REACH PAST 10 TO 20 MPH COMPLETE MONTH 3

YOU WILL BE SERVING HARDER THAN EVER BEFORE! MAKE SURE TO WARM UP BEFORE AND STRETCH AFTER TRAINING TO PREVENT INJURIES.

CONGRATS YOU SHOULD BE PAST 20 MPH FROM YOUR ORIGINAL SERVICE SPEED.

THE 3 STAGES OF THE SUPERMAN SERVE

DURING COMPETITION

This would be when you are competing against other tennis players and are doing additional serves during competition besides this program.

DURING OFF SEASON

This is the stage when you are not competing at all and can work as hard as you want without sacrificing match results.

PRE-COMPETITION

This is the stage when you are preparing for competition and need to be at your best. This could be 1, 2, or 3 months before an event.

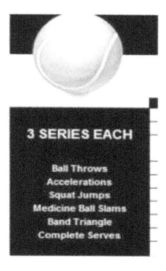

These are the 6 exercises you will be performing during the training. You must perform 3 series of each.

MONDAY		
Serve Harder Training		
Repetitions		
Beg.	Interm.	Adv.
6	8	10
10	10	10
5	7	10
5	8	10
10	10	10
10	15	20

MONDAY		
Serve Harder Training		
Repetitions		
Beg.	Interm.	Adv.
REST		

This is the description of a training session for Monday on one week and the following week. The first Monday is divided into Beginner, Intermediate, and advanced. Below you will see how many repetitions you must complete depending on your level. The Monday below represents a resting day in which you do not perform any serve training.

SUNDAY		
Serve Harder Training		
Repetitions		
Beg.	Interm.	Adv.
TOURNAMENT OR SERVES		
ONLY 1 SERIES		
30	50	80

This is an example of a weekend day when you might have a tournament. In that case you would not practice serves. If, on the other hand, you do not have competition on that day, you would perform only one series of serves based on your level of play.

MONTH 1

THURSDAY

Serve Harder Training

	Repetitions	
Beg.	Interm.	Adv.
	REST	

MONTH 2

THURSDAY

Serve Harder Training

	Repetitions	
Beg.	Interm.	Adv.
8	10	12
12	12	12
7	9	12
6	8	12
12	12	12
10	15	20

This part of the chart shows MONTH 1 and MONTH 2. Make sure you do not skip months and follow the charts as directed.

This part in one of the charts shows entire weeks´ training with all respective rest days. On rest days you should rest your shoulder so that you can continue working hard on the following training day.

PART 3

SIX TIPS TO A FASTER SERVE

TIP # 1

IMPACT THE BALL OUT IN FRONT OF THE BASELINE

No serve will ever reach maximum velocity of you are hitting the ball behind you. Even though you might feel comfortable doing things the wrong way, it's still the wrong way and needs to be corrected. Old routines need to be replaced with newer and better routines. This is how you will reach your full potential. After completing a serve your whole body should have landed passed the baseline which can only mean you tossed the ball out in front of you. By throwing your body out in front of you when you serve will not only prevent injuries but will also generate much more force than just your arm by itself. Most serve injuries happen because of a bad toss, and that's usually behind your ideal point of contact.

TIP #2

WRIST PRONATION

Most people never notice one of the most important elements to a fast serve. There are two stages the ball goes through after you serve: the first is after impact, the ball goes at an initial speed upon impact in the air, and the second is the speed the ball goes after impacting the ground on your opponents' side. One of two things can happen here: either your serve hits the ground and starts to lose speed as is most common, or the ball hits the ground and maintains or increases speed. How is this possible? This is where wrist pronation comes into play. Right when you are snapping your wrist at impact with the ball you want to snap your wrist down and to the left so that your racquet face is perpendicular to the court (with your right thumb aiming down to the court, if you are a righty) instead of facing it and then bring that arm down to your opposite hip. You can watch some of our instructional serve technique videos for free as a bonus for purchasing this product by going to tennisvideostore.com.

TIP #3

CONNECT YOUR FEET WITH YOUR HANDS

In order to generate any real power you must use your entire body. The starting point is your feet. Practice adding a stronger jump beginning with your legs. Experiment with different types of jumps, either with your feet together, apart, or coming together as you prepare for impact and see which one helps you push off the ground the hardest. The one that allows you the jump the highest or push the hardest will be the type of jump that will allow you to increase your hand speed as every serve is a chain reaction that has a beginning and an end. It all starts with your legs.

TIP #4

SOUND BIOMECHANICS

Serve biomechanics are the basis for a good serve. It basically means how efficiently your body connects with every other part to create a smooth and effortless service motion. Having good technique on your serve is the only way you will reach serve speeds passed 100 mph. Make sure you have a good coach to go over it with you. This training program includes one-on-one coaching so make sure ask questions and get the most out of it.

TIP #5

KEEP YOU HEAD AND CHIN UP

By keeping your head and chin up during the service motion you promote two very important things: first you allow yourself to watch the ball longer which will allow you to impact the ball cleaner which will equal a faster serve immediately, and second, it will help you to keep your left arm up so that you can use it to pull down at the right moment and generate good body rotation. Good form is essential. Make sure you remind yourself to keep your head up by keeping your left arm up (if you are right handed and the opposite if you are left handed) as long as possible to maintain a good frame of body.

TIP #6

IMPACT THE BALL ON THE HIGHEST PART OF THE STRINGS

Most people probably never check to see where they are impacting the ball on their strings and so miss out on the potential to add more mph´s to their serve. You should always strive to hit the ball on the high part of your strings as to create the most leverage on your swing. Low contact on the strings will never generate as much acceleration as a ball that is impacted on the high part of the racquet. Check to see where most tennis ball hairs are left on your racquet and work to find the ideal point upon impact. Keep working at it until you find this spot. Also, creating a larger circle with your swing by reaching your arm out is also part of this concept of leverage so make sure you don´t impact the ball with a tight or completely straight elbow. Stay relaxed and swing freely through the ball. Using leverage as a tool to increase the speed of your serve will allow you to achieve results faster.

12 More Tennis Tips to Improve Your Game

Tip #1: Toss the ball higher on your serve

Most people blame their hitting arm for their mistakes but the majority of the time it has nothing to do with your swinging arm. It's all about the tossing arm.
The key elements for a good toss are:

- Keep your tossing arm relaxed and make sure you hold the ball gently. You should be holding the ball with your finger tips and not with the palm of your hand.

- Work on placing the ball in the air instead of tossing the ball in the air. This will make your toss more precise and consistent.

- The best place to toss the ball is always about a foot out in front of your right shoulder if you were facing the court and serving a slice or flat serve. If you are serving a kick serve you should be tossing the ball behind your head or above your head, depending on how much arc you create with your back.

You should practice your toss at least 30 times before hitting an actual ball and at least 3 times per week.

If you have a bad toss you will never have a good serve so start paying more attention to your tossing arm if you want to improve your serve.

Tip #2: Split step before every shot

Some people think their slowness requires more sprints or 5 miles runs but they don't know it's more about training smarter and not harder.

The "split step" is nothing more than a hop with both feet to help you prepare for your opponents shot. Make sure they remain about at shoulders distance apart to help you stay low.

The "split step" can be done with a low and quick hop or a high and slow hop depending on how fast the point is going. Go fast and short for quick rallies and points. Slow and high for high bouncing topspin shots and longer, slower rallies.

When should you be doing the "split step"?

Well there's a precise moment when you should do the hop. You should split step right when your opponent is making contact with the ball as to react the quickest to any direction that may be require of you.

How do practice the split step?

Jumping rope with both feet at the same time helps build strength and stamina so that you don't get tired of doing it during your match.

You can also stand at the base line and practice hopping back and forth with both feet at the same time while keeping your feet about shoulder distance apart.

Doing plyometric or jump training is very effective as well to help you improve your split step and over all jumping ability. The important thing here is to do the training over a soft surface and not overdo it or your knees will pay the price.

Tip #3: Invest more time on your point of contact

Everyone thinks their looking at the ball, and they are, but not the way it should be done to make clean contact.

Do you ever take the time to notice that all the posters of tennis pros always show them watching the ball when they make contact?

Well, that's because they know just how important it is to them and their game.

The secret is in learning to invest more time and keep your eyes on the ball at the point of contact and not look away too quick at its destination. Once you've hit the ball there's nothing you can do to make it steer down into the court. All that matters is the moment you make contact.

Try these techniques to help you invest more time on your point of contact:

- when making contact with the ball try to see

what number the ball has on it. It sounds crazy but don't think it's impossible. You can search for markings on the ball as well but trying to see what number is on the ball is enough of a challenge.

- try watching your racquets shadow as you swing when you make contact to determine if your racquet is angled correctly as to make the ball go in the right direction. For some people this might be a straight racquet while others might have a tilted racquet for top spin or slice.

When you swing your racquet your eyes will never be fast enough to see it still but you can see the shadow or silhouette it creates when you swing it and this is what you want to focus on to help you keep your eyes on the pint of contact.

- A difficult but fun exercise is having someone feed you some balls while you hit the ball but you will not be allowed to see where it is going. You can only focus on where you hit on the ball. Bottom, top, side or middle is what you want to be able to reply every time you hit the ball. At the beginning it will be hard to resist not watching where the balls lands and if it goes in or out but with practice it will become easier and easier.

Tip #4: Follow through on all your ground strokes

Under pressure we all shorten our swing thinking it will help make the ball stay inside the lines more often but the exact opposite is true.

Following through is necessary to complete your tennis stroke. Completing a half swing will only give you half as good a shot.

More importantly, repeating the wrong to swing (not following through) will only encourage you to do the same in a match situation or under pressure.

Most people follow a similar pattern of shortening their swing more and more the greater their stress level is. In order to change this you want to start making it a habit of following through always, on all your ground strokes and serve.

A good drill you can practice to improve you follow through is to mark an "X" on both elbows and when begin hitting some balls. Your practice partner or coach should be able to see the "X" every time you finish your swing and this way proving you have followed through on your shot. This is a great drill for players who want to improve their follow through in pressure situations.

Tip #5: Work on serve consistency to win more often

Serving an ace and then a double fault will simply leave you right where you started. Back to even and that's not the goal.

The secret to improving consistency on your serve is to start with a slow speed and gradually work your way to faster speeds as you become more and more consistent.

Being able to reduce the amount of double faults you make in a match can have a serious effect on your match results. Winning an extra game or two versus giving them away in the form of a double fault can mean winning more matches.

The basic elements to improving serve consistency are:

- adding some spin to your serve to add control and direction.

- repeat the same motion over and over. Don't try to hit the ball harder and harder and don't change up your serves so often that you can't get a slice or flat serve in because you are varying them too often.

- don't rush. Bounce the ball more often and breathe before serving to help you slow down. Serving is not a race it's about get it in as often as possible!

Tip #6: Return more serves with better footwork

Your feet are connected to your hands and brain. The better your footwork is, the better your hands and brain will react as well.

When you stand at the baseline to return serve it's like starting an engine. That engine needs to get warmed up before going at maximum capacity. The best way to get your body ready to return serve is get your feet moving. Hopping, jumping, alternating leg jumps and jump rope jumps are all good starting points.

The worst thing you can do to return serve is stand flat on your feet so make sure to be on your toes or at least the front of your feet.

Move forward on your return of serve as to turn your body into a moving wall in which the ball will knock into when you hit the ball.

Split stepping and moving around before returning serve is the best thing you can do and will definitely help return more serves no matter how hard or with how much spin they come with.

Tip #7: Warm up well before the match starts to begin successfully

Getting a jump start on the match makes all the difference in the world and especially in your first set results.

Most people have a very light warm up which includes: stretching, signing with the tournament director or referee, greeting friends, and heading on over to the court to start their match.

The right way to warm up before your match would be to:

- do dynamic stretches to get the whole body ready for about 15 minutes (or longer if you feel you need more).

- jog around the court a few times in all direction: forward, sideways, and backwards to loosen up your legs and feet.

- have a light hit with someone you feel comfortable with. Make sure to practice all shots you feel you might be using against your opponent. Basic shots that should always be warmed up are: forehand, backhand, volleys, overhead, and serve. More advanced shots you can warm up and might use are: angled forehands and backhands, drop shots, slice, top spin lobs, etc.

- do a light band warm up if you have been doing bands as part of your warm up but if you have not done bands before, don't start before your match.

- check your bag to make sure you have something to drink, extra grips, towel, extra shirt, extra socks, a healthy snack, etc.

Tip #8: Stretch after every match to be ready for your next opponent

After winning your match you will probably have to play your second match within the next 48 hours which means the looser you are, the better you will perform in the matches to follow.

Learn to make it part of your routine, no matter what the results of your match are, to stretch after every match. Sometimes if you win you might decide to celebrate and skip stretching because you won and don't need to stretch. Other time you lose and decide not to even bother with stretching since you lost your match and now it makes no difference as you don't have a next opponent today, tomorrow or all week.

The right way to approach this habit is to understand that getting better at tennis requires ongoing improvement that does not have happen in one day or week. It takes time to slowly develop your game and to do so you have make sure all the pieces of the puzzle are being worked on as often as possible. One of the most important pieces of the puzzle includes your overall mobility which entails becoming more agile and flexible. The best time stretch is when you are very warm and have worked up a sweat. That's why you should do it after your matches.

Tip #9: Work every point of the match, especially the first points of very game

Do you ever ask yourself what is the most important point of the match? Well it's every point since there all worth the same. You just have to accumulate enough of them to win the match.

Some points matter more because of the score or the moment in which they are being played.

To get a head start in most tennis matches make it a priority to work extra hard on the first points of every game to begin string in each and every game.

The odds will always be in your favor when you start winning in every first few points of each game and especially after you win the first set. It is said that most people who win the first set win the match 70% of the time which tells you the importance of winning the first set and doing it from the first point on.

A lot of times, starting with a 15-0 or 30-0

advantage in every game gives a mental edge that your opponent cannot deny and will give up many times thinking is far behind in the score. This will be reflected many times with silly unforced errors or way to aggressive points.

Work every point of the match and see how it does wonders for your game and how you will even surprise yourself with wins that you did not expect.

Tip #10: Close out matches decisively before it's too late

Having trouble winning? Well it might be because you can't do the most necessary of things to win a tennis match. Close it out!

The most difficult thing in a tennis match is many times closing it out. If you can't close a match out, you will never win any matches or tournaments. The truth is, you learn a lot from your losses but you learn to enjoy the game through winning matches.

Winning and closing out matches is important so let's go over some very important things to do when you the chance to close out a match.

First, figure out what you have been doing to win points in the match as you will probably have a much higher chance at winning match point dot exactly what it you there.

Second, don't let your body freeze. Keep your feet moving and your head up high no matter how tired you are.

Third, stay positive! If your opponent hits an impossible shot and you couldn't do anything about it, don't stress about or get discouraged. How many impossible shots do you think they can hit in a row? Not enough to keep you from winning match point.

Four, learn not to rush on match point. Most errors and bad decisions happen when you rush. Take your time and do things at your own pace even if your opponent complains you are going too slowly.

Lastly, learn to transfer the pressure on to your opponent by bringing then to the net and forcing them to volley or simply pass them. Overheads are highly dreaded shots to hit under pressure as well. You can also rush the net on their weaker side and force them to pass you instead of playing it safe.

Tip #11: Stay positive no matter what the score or situation of the match

Losing one point, or two or even a whole game is not enough reason to throw the rest of the set or match away due to negativity.

Too often I see the younger players lose important points or a set and then give the next set. This loss of temper or patience needs to be corrected with positive thinking and conviction that they still have a good chance at winning the match.

More and more often professional tennis players are hiring sports psychologists to help them with their mental toughness simply because they understand just how much this aspect of their game can mean to them. Most of the time professional athletes are taught to stay positive under pressure situations. No matter where the pressure comes from.

Some of the best ways to train yourself to stay positive are:

- Write down on a stick "stay positive" or "don't

give up" or "keep fighting" and stick it on the
inside of your racquet where you can see it often.
The inside of the neck of the racquet just above
the grip is usually the best place. This will remind
you what you need to be doing.

- Maintain a positive image of yourself. How you
carry yourself will reflect how your opponent sees
you and they should see you with: your head up,
shoulders back, moving your feet, straight back,
etc.

- One change overs put your towel over your head
and forget about everything and simply breathe.
Once you put the towel back down and stand up
reflect the image of a champion as if you have
already won the match.

Tip #12: Use your brain to win more matches and develop your mental toughness

The most important muscle in your body is usually the most under used but it shouldn't have to be that way.

Your brain can be your greatest ally or your worst enemy. Know how to use it can benefit every player at every level. Learn to improve your focus, concentration, calmness, thought process, staying positive.

Try these techniques:

- Use positive key words like: you can do, keep going, now's your opportunity, get the serve in, just keep running, one more point, and keep your head up.

- Use positive body language to program your brain towards success.

- Keep your mind and eyes on the ball and on your

court only.

- Work more on consistency as it is one of the best ways to increase your concentration capacity and focus. Winning one point is good but winning the match requires more than one point.

- Breathe in between points, during points and on change overs. Don't hold your breath as your brain needs oxygen to work and to stay focused.

- Work on visual training to help your eyes stay focused on the ball.

- Practice some pre-match visualization to help you prepare for what you need to be doing on the court later or the next day. For some people this is incredibly powerful so give it a try. Visualize your match and points and shots you want to do in your mind so that your body knows what to do.

15 BONUS SERVE DRILLS TO MASTER CONSISTENCY, SPIN, AND POWER

1. Higher First Serve Percentage Drill

Make sure you warm up first before hitting hard serves. First serves can be served flat, with slice, or with kick or topspin depending on what your preferred style of play is so you don't necessarily have to just hit flat and hard. Often players that play on clay use what's called a three quarters serve. This is simply a very fast second serve which is normally done with spin but taking a lot more risk on it.

Start serving on the deuce side of the court. You are going to serve and when the ball lands on the service box you are going to call that "1 first serve in a row". The next serve you hit should go in for you to call it "2 first serves in a row" but if you miss your serve you simply go back to zero. The goal is to get to the highest number of consecutive first serves in. If for any reason you are 10 or 15 serves and miss, you must go back to zero as that is how this drill is done. Once you feel you have reached the highest number possible, you will switch to the ad side of the court and do the same, Switching serving sides is very important since most people serve better off one side than the other but you can only determine this by making sure you give yourself a chance on both sides to determine your highest number possible.

This drill will help you improve your first serve percentages which will normally get more free points in your match. Remember to right done what your highest number was on each side so that you can go back and try to improve off that number the following day or week.

2. Higher Second Serve Percentage Drill

The second serve percentage drill is very simple. You're going to start on the deuce side of the court. Begin by serving a second serve and if the serve goes in count "1 second serve in a row". When you get to two serves in a row count "2 second serves in a row". If you miss a serve you must go back to zero. Your goal is to reach the highest number possible as to improve your confidence under pressure and become more consistent.

Once you're done serving on the deuce side switch to the ad side of the court and serve from there. Switching is important so that you can figure out on which side you serve better. Most people have a stronger side or a favorite side. Write down your highest number for both sides and then try to improve off that number every time you practice serves.

3. Match Preparation Drill

You're going to play a match against yourself and without an opponent on the other side of the court. Begin by serving two serves. A first serve and a second serve. If you get your second serve in you don't have to serve a second serve, just like in a real match. If you get your first serve in you count "15-0" and move on to the ad side as you would normally do in a real tennis match. If you miss your first serve you should serve a second serve. If the serve goes in you would count it as a point but if you miss your second serve you count that point against you as you would normally "0-15". Count just like a normal match. Once you finish the first game, move on to the second game. Your goal is to finish winning the set by reaching 6 games just like a normal match. If you win 6-0 then you should on to the next two drills described below but if you win 6-4 or lose 3-6, you should spend more time on this drill before

moving on to the next two drills below.

4. Match Preparation Drill for First Serves

You're going to play a match against yourself and without an opponent on the other side of the court. Begin by serving two serves. A first serve and another first serve in replacement of a second serve. If you get your first serve in you don't have to serve a second serve, just like in a real match. If you get your first serve in you count "15-0" and move on to the ad side as you would normally do in a real tennis match. If you miss your first serve you should serve a second serve (which for this drill be another first serve). If the serve goes in you would count it as a point but if you miss your second serve you count that point against you as you would normally "0-15". Count just like a normal match. Once you finish the first game, move on to the second game. Your goal is to finish winning the set by reaching 6 games just like a normal match but by only serving first serves, even when you are supposed to serve a second serve.

This drill will greatly improve your first serve percentage under pressure and in a match.

5. Match Preparation Drill for Second Serves

You're going to play a match against yourself and without an opponent on the other side of the court. Begin by serving two serves. A second serve (instead of a first serve) and another second serve. If you get your first serve in you don't have to serve a second serve, just like in a real match. If you get your first serve in you count "15-0" and move on to the ad side as you would normally do in a real tennis match. If you miss your first serve you should serve a second serve (which for this drill be another serve). If the serve goes in you would count it as a point but if you miss your second serve you count that point against you as you would normally "0-15". Count just like a normal match. Once you finish the first game, move on to the second game. Your goal is to finish winning the set by reaching 6 games just like a normal match but by only serving second serves, even when you are supposed to serve a first serve.

This drill will greatly improve your second serve percentage under pressure and in a match.

6. The Side to Side Drill

For this drill you want to start by serving from the deuce side of the court. Start by serving out wide and then switch and serve down the middle or also known as the "center T". Alternate each time you hit a ball so that you never serve to the same side. Once you hit 30-100 balls on the deuce side of the court switch and do the same on the other side. The amount of serves you hit is determined by your level of play and also by how many serves you can hit without hurting your shoulder, especially if you have had shoulder problems in the past.

7. The 3-in-1 Serve Drill

For this drill you want to start by serving from the deuce side of the court. You will serve to the three common spots in the service box: out wide, to the body, and down the middle or center "T". Begin by serving out wide first, then make your next serve go to your opponents body, and the last or third ball you serve should go down the middle or center of the court. You're going to repeat the pattern every time to improve your aim.

Once you hit 30-100 balls on the deuce side of the court switch and do the same on the other side. The amount of serves you hit is determined by your level of play and also by how many serves you can hit without hurting your shoulder, especially if you have had shoulder problems in the past.

8. The Going Forward Serve Drill

Start by placing a cone about 4-6 feet from the service line in front of where ever you decide to stand when you serve. You will need to serve and then run forward towards the cone and run around it in a counter-clockwise motion and always facing the other side of the court so you never run turning around. When you return back to the service line, take another ball and do it again. The goal is to start making contact more out in front and past the service line as to benefit from being closer to your target which will always be the service box on the opposite side of the court. This drill will help you do many positive things for your serve:

1. It will improve your toss.

2. It will help you to fully reach forward when making contact so that your arm isn't restricted or tucked in when hitting the ball.

3. The drill will teach you to use your whole body not just your arm to generate power.

4. It will also improve your net game as you will be constantly moving towards the net.

5. You will learn to hit down into the court and not upwards to the other side of the court.

6. Your chin will remain up longer than usual which will get you more balls over the net.

Once you hit 30-100 balls on the deuce side of the court switch and do the same on the other side. The amount of serves you hit is determined by your level of play and also by how many serves you can hit without hurting your shoulder, especially if you have had shoulder problems in the past.

9. Serve and Volley Drill

For the serve and volley drill you need to start on the service line. Start by serving and moving forward towards the net. You will need to complete an imaginary volley on the forehand side. I like to call this a simulated volley since you are not going to make contact with any ball on that shot but you will need to use your best technique and effort on it so that you don't just rush through it. The key is to make sure you cross the mid court line before you volley so that you have gone all the way to the net. This is a very physically demanding drill but is worth the effort.

Do this 10-50 times on the deuce side of the court and splitting the serves between half forehand volleys and half backhand volleys when you come into the net. You can add an overhead after the volley which will even further improve your serve and volley game. Total serves would be 30-100 serves on the deuce side.

Once you hit 30-100 balls on the deuce side of the court switch and do the same on the other side. The amount of serves you hit is determined by your level of play and also by how many serves you can hit without hurting your shoulder, especially if you have had shoulder problems in the past.

10. The Three-Quarters Serve Drill

For the three-quarters serve drill you want to stand on the service line on the deuce side of the court. You will need to serve a fast second serve as to still have some form of control and consistency over the serve but be a lot more aggressive with it. It should be a serve that gives your opponent trouble to return but should not necessarily be an ace. The best way to do this is with a slice or kick serve but can still be done just flat if you don't have any spin serves.

Once you hit 30-100 balls on the deuce side of the court switch and do the same on the other side. The amount of serves you hit is determined by your level of play and also by how many serves you can hit without hurting your shoulder, especially if you have had shoulder problems in the past.

11. The "Move Around the Baseline" Serve Drill

For this drill you will need to stand on the deuce side of the service line and start as close to the middle as possible. You will serve from that spot and then take step to the right and serve again. You will repeat this until you get to the doubles alley. At that moment you will begin serving by taking a step to the left as to move back to the middle of the court. Do not rush when doing this drill. Complete a serve and then step to the side and complete the next serve so that you get used to serving from different angles on the baseline.

Once you hit 30-100 balls on the deuce side of the court switch and do the same on the other side. The amount of serves you hit is determined by your level of play and also by how many serves you can hit without feeling fatigued.

12. The Variety Serve Drill

For this drill you will need to know how to serve flat, with slice, and with topspin or kick serve in order to perform it. For this drill you will begin by standing on the deuce side of the court and you will start serving a flat serve followed by a slice serve followed by a topspin or kick serve. This order is important but not strict since you can go from a flat serve to a kick serve without a problem and then to a slice serve. The key here is variety. You are not allowed to serve the same serve in a row. You must mix each serve after hitting the last one. This will help you win many more serves and have more service winners because of the difficulty level it will give your opponent. Mixing serves will benefit you more than just being predictable.

Once you hit 30-100 balls on the deuce side of the court switch and do the same on the other side.

The amount of serves you hit is determined by your level of play and also by how many serves you can hit without hurting your shoulder, especially if you have had shoulder problems in the past.

Serve flat, slice, top spin serves in that order for 30 balls in a row.

13. Power Serve Training Drill

For this drill you want to start by serving from the deuce side of the court. You will begin by serving soft in order to slow bring up the serve speed every time you serve a ball. The first serve you hit should go very slow, the second should go a little faster, etc. When you get to your sixth serve hit, having started soft on serve 1, you should be hitting your hardest. Repeat this process three times going from slow to fast as to warm up you serve and to figure out what you hardest or fastest serve is. Once you know just how hard you can serve you will only serve hard until you hit 20-60 balls on the deuce side of the court switch and do the same on the other side. The amount of serves you hit is determined by your level of play and also by how many serves you can hit without hurting your shoulder, especially if you have had shoulder problems in the past.

Make sure for this drill that you still try to maintain as good technique as possible so that you're now just going for power and losing what's most important for your serve, which is smoothness. Having a smooth and relaxed serve will get you a much faster serve and doing it with proper technique will make it much more possible to do it effectively.

14. The Short Court Serve Drill

For this drill you want to start by serving from the deuce side of the court but now you will stand on the mid-court line. Your goal is to serve into the service box as you normally would but now you will be standing much closer inside the court. You are allowed to toss the ball and make contact as out in front of you as you want without foot-faulting. Complete 20 serves from both the deuce and ad sides. Write down how many of your serves landed in and if the second bounce hit the back fence or if it did not reach the back fence. For advanced players, measure just how high on the back fence you hit and work on getting it to reach higher every time.

After completing 20 serves on each side while standing right before the mid-court line, take a step back and serve a ball into the service box.

Next, take another step back and serve again. Slowly continue taking a step back every time you finish serving until you reach the baseline which is where you will stay once reaching that spot on the court. When you reach the baseline serve 20 more serves from there on both the deuce and ad sides of the court. Once you reach the baseline remember to aim higher on your serve since your serves might tend to go to the net at first because of the angle at which your racquet got used to hitting at when you were at the mid-court line.

15. The On-Your-Knees Serve Drill

For this drill you will need a comfortable mat or towel that will not give your knees any pain if you kneel on it. Begin by kneeling on the mat while being right on the baseline on the deuce side of the court. Take a ball and serve into the service box. You will complete a normal serve except the lower half of your body will be eliminated since you will be on your knees. Complete 10-20 serves while on your knees, then stand up and do 10-20 normal serves without the mat. This is your first round of serves. Go back down on your knees and begin the second round of serves. The combination should be a round of serves on your knees followed by a round of normal standing serves. Repeat this process 3 times to complete one side of the court. You should have served 30-60 serves on the deuce side by the time you are done. Once you are done with the deuce side move the mat to the ad side and start the process all over again. By the end of this drill you should have completed 60-120 serves. The amount of serves will depend on you comfort level and just how hard you decide to work that day.

CAUTION: Do not complete all the drills above on the same day as you are not supposed to do 1,000 serves in a day or training session. Choose one or two at a maximum for a day or training session and work on those. All of these drill are great and will improve your serve simply choose the ones that you want to do and spread them out during the week or month to get the most out of these 15 drills. Make sure you have someone take a look at your overall technique since that is most important in having a successful serve and will help you reach your potential faster. Stretch and warm up before starting to serve. Jumping rope, jogging, doing ball throws, and doing arm circles are all good ways to warm up before serving.

TENNIS NUTRITION: POWER SHAKES FOR TENNIS

1. Oat & Almond Shake

Preparing time: 5 minutes
Servings: 3

1. *Ingredients:*

220ml milk
1 tablespoon almonds (grinded) (15g)
1 tablespoon oats (15g)
1 teaspoon maple syrup (5g)
½ teaspoon vanilla extract (2-3g)
2 tablespoon Greek Yogurt (30g)
30g whey protein

2. *Preparation:*

All ingredients go in a blender and are blend until the consistence is smooth.

3. *Nutritional facts (amount per 100ml/entire composition):*

Contains calcium, iron;
Calories: 111

Calories from Fat: 29

Total Fat: 3.2g
   Saturated
   Fat: 0.7g

Cholesterol: 21mg
Sodium: 58mg

Potassium: 182mg

Total Carbohydrates:
   9.3g
   Dietary Fiber: 0.8g
   Sugar: 5.1g
Protein: 11.1g
Calories: 333

   Calories from Fat:
   86

Total Fat: 9.5g

   Saturated Fat:
   2.1g

Cholesterol: 64mg

Sodium: 175mg

Potassium: 547mg

Total Carbohydrates:
27.9g
   Dietary Fiber: 2.6g
   Sugar: 15.3g
Protein: 33.5g

2. Peppermint Oatmeal Shake
Preparing time: 5 minutes
Servings: 5

1. Ingredients:

70g oatmeal
30g bran flakes
300ml milk
50g quark
½ teaspoon peppermint extract (3g)
30g ice-cream (vanilla/chocolate)
50g whey protein (chocolate)

2. Preparation:

Mix all ingredients in a blender until the composition is smooth.

3. Nutritional facts (amount per 100ml/entire composition):

Contains Vitamin A, calcium, iron.

Calories: 180
   Calories from Fat: 51

Total Fat: 5.6g
   Saturated Fat: 2.9g

Cholesterol: 30mg
Sodium: 111mg

Potassium: 179mg

Total Carbohydrates: 20.7g

Dietary Fiber: 2.5g

Sugar: 6.2g

Protein: 12.6g

Calories: 900

Calories from Fat: 253

Total Fat: 28.1g

Saturated Fat: 14.4g

Cholesterol: 151mg

Sodium: 555mg

Potassium: 869mg

Total Carbohydrates: 104g

Dietary Fiber: 12.4g

Sugar: 31.2g

Protein: 63.2g

3. Cinnamon Shake
Preparing time: 5 minutes
Servings: 3

1. Ingredients:

240ml milk
¼ tablespoon cinnamon (4g)
½ teaspoon vanilla extracts (3g)
2 tablespoon vanilla ice-cream (30g)
2 tablespoon oats (30g)
50g whey protein

2. Preparation:

Mix all ingredients in a blender until the composition is smooth.

3. Nutritional facts (amount per 100g/entire composition):

Contains Vitamin A, calcium, iron.

Calories: 131
    Calories from Fat: 30

Total Fat: 3.3g
    Saturated Fat: 1.8g

Cholesterol: 42mg
Sodium: 73mg

Potassium: 158mg

Total Carbohydrates: 10.3g
    Dietary Fiber: 1g

Sugar: 4.8g

Protein: 15.3g

Calories: 342

Calories from Fat: 89

Total Fat: 9.9g

Saturated Fat: 5.4g

Cholesterol: 127mg

Sodium: 219mg

Potassium: 474mg

Total Carbohydrates: 31g

Dietary Fiber: 3.1g

Sugar: 14.4g

Protein: 45.9g

4. Almonds Shake
Preparing time: 5 minutes
Servings: 5

1. *Ingredients:*

220ml almond milk
120g oatmeal
50g whey protein
80g raisins
20g almonds (grinded)
1 tablespoon peanut butter (15g)

2. *Preparation:*

Mix all ingredients in a blender until the composition is smooth.

3. *Nutritional facts (amount per 100g/entire composition):*

Contains : Vitamin C, iron, calcium.

Calories: 241
   Calories from Fat: 61

Total Fat: 6.7g
   Saturated Fat: 1.6g

Cholesterol: 24mg
Sodium: 57mg

Potassium: 339mg

Total Carbohydrates: 33.8g
   Dietary Fiber: 3.7g

Sugar: 12.5g

Protein: 13.9g

Calories: 1207

Calories from Fat: 304

Total Fat: 33.7g

Saturated Fat: 8g

Cholesterol: 122mg

Sodium: 283mg

Potassium: 1693mg

Total Carbohydrates: 169g

Dietary Fiber: 18.5g

Sugar: 62.3g

Protein: 69.4g

5. Banana & Almonds Shake
Preparing time: 5 minutes
Servings: 5

1. Ingredients:

2 bananas
230ml almond milk
20g almonds (grinded)
10g pistachios (grinded)
40g whey protein

2. Preparation:

Mix all ingredients in a blender until the composition is smooth.

3. Nutritional facts (amount per 100g/entire composition):

Contains Vitamin A, C, iron, calcium.

Calories: 241
  Calories from Fat: 61

Total Fat: 6.7g
  Saturated Fat: 1.6g

Cholesterol: 24mg
Sodium: 57mg

Potassium: 339mg

Total Carbohydrates: 33.8g

Dietary Fiber: 3.7g
Sugar: 12.5g
Protein: 13.9g
Calories: 1073

Calories from Fat:
659

Total Fat: 73.2g

Saturated Fat:
52.1g

Cholesterol: 83mg

Sodium: 109mg

Potassium: 1934mg

Total Carbohydrates:
78.7g
Dietary Fiber:
14.8g
Sugar: 39.4g
Protein: 42.8g

6. Wild Berry Shake

Preparing time: 5 minutes
Servings: 7

1. Ingredients:

30g strawberries
30g blueberries
30g raspberries
30g currants
500ml milk
60g whey protein
1 teaspoon vanilla extract (5g)
1 teaspoon lemon extract (5g)

2. Preparation:

Mix all ingredients in a blender until the composition is smooth. You can also add some ice cubes to the mix.

3. Nutritional facts (amount per 100g/entire composition):

Contains Vitamin A, C, iron, calcium.

Calories: 78

Calories from Fat: 19

Total Fat: 2.1g

Saturated Fat: 1.2g

Cholesterol: 24mg
Sodium: 50mg

Potassium: 119mg

Total Carbohydrates:
6.7g
Dietary Fiber: 0.7g
Sugar: 4.7g
Protein: 8.7g
Calories: 549

Calories from Fat:
131

Total Fat: 14.6g

Saturated Fat:
8.1g

Cholesterol: 167mg

Sodium: 351mg

Potassium: 832mg

Total Carbohydrates:
46.9g
Dietary Fiber: 4.6g
Sugar: 33g
Protein: 61g

7. Strawberry Shake

Preparing time: 5 minutes
Servings: 5

1. *Ingredients:*

30g strawberries
100g Greek Yogurt
200ml milk
40g whey protein
2 eggs
20g sweetener (honey/ brown sugar)
ice cubes
1 teaspoon vanilla extract (5g)

2. *Preparation:*

Mix all ingredients in a blender until the composition is smooth.

The Greek Yogurt can have different aromas like vanilla or strawberry, or just be plain yogurt. It works will all flavors.

3. *Nutritional facts (amount per 100g/entire composition):*

Contains Vitamin A, C, iron, calcium.
Calories: 96

Calories from Fat: 32

Total Fat: 3.5g
Saturated
Fat: 1.6g

Cholesterol: 87mg
Sodium: 65mg

Potassium: 131mg

Total Carbohydrates:
9.2g
Dietary Fiber: 2.5g
Sugar: 3.4g
Protein: 11.3g

Calories: 508

Calories from Fat: 157

Total Fat: 17.4g

Saturated Fat: 8g

Cholesterol: 433mg

Sodium: 326mg

Potassium: 656mg

Total Carbohydrates:
45.9g
Dietary Fiber:
12.4g
Sugar: 17.2g
Protein: 56.6g

8. Strawberry Vanilla Shake

Preparing time: 5 minutes
Servings: 7

1. Ingredients:

100g strawberries
1 banana
1 teaspoon vanilla extract (5g)
1 tablespoon strawberries extract (15g)
50g oats
200ml milk
5 eggs
Ice cubes

2. Preparation:

Mix all ingredients in a blender until the composition is smooth.

3. Nutritional facts (amount per 100g/entire composition):

Contains Vitamin A, C, iron, calcium.

Calories: 112
Calories from Fat: 39
Total Fat: 4.3g
Saturated Fat: 1.4g
Cholesterol: 119mg
Sodium: 59mg

Potassium: 170mg

Total Carbohydrates:
   11.7g
   Dietary Fiber: 1.4g
   Sugar: 4.6g
Protein: 6.1g

Calories: 782

   Calories from Fat:
   271

Total Fat: 30.1g

Saturated Fat:
10.1g

Cholesterol: 835mg

Sodium: 421mg

Potassium: 1189mg

Total Carbohydrates:
   82g
   Dietary Fiber:
   10.1g
   Sugar: 32.5g
Protein: 43g

9. Strawberry & Nuts Shake

Preparing time: 5 minutes

Servings: 4

1. Ingredients:

50g strawberries

50g mix nuts (chopped)

200ml milk

100g Greek yogurt

2 tablespoon oats (30g)

2. Preparation:

Mix all ingredients in a blender until the composition is smooth.

3. Nutritional facts (amount per 100g/entire composition):

Contains Vitamin A, C, iron, calcium.

Calories: 140

Calories from Fat: 81

Total Fat: 9g

Saturated Fat: 1.4g

Cholesterol: 1mg

Sodium: 80mg

Potassium: 125mg

Total Carbohydrates: 9.2g

Dietary Fiber: 1.4g

Sugar: 4.3g

Protein: 6.9g

Calories: 417

    Calories from Fat: 324

Total Fat: 36g

    Saturated Fat: 5.4g

Cholesterol: 5mg

Sodium: 321mg

Potassium: 499mg

Total Carbohydrates: 36.9g
    Dietary Fiber: 5.5g
    Sugar: 17.1g
Protein: 27.6g

10. Raspberry Shake
Preparing time: 5 minutes
Servings: 4

1. Ingredients:

50g whey protein
100g raspberries
30g strawberries
50g sour cream
200ml milk
1 teaspoon lime extract (5g)

2. Preparation:

Mix all ingredients in a blender until the composition is smooth.

3. Nutritional facts (amount per 100g/entire composition):

Contains Vitamin A, C, B-12, iron, calcium.

Calories: 116
 Calories from Fat: 41

Cholesterol: 36mg
Sodium: 54mg

Potassium: 168mg

Total Fat: 4.6g
 Saturated Fat: 2.6g

Total Carbohydrates: 8.1g
 Dietary Fiber: 1.8g

Sugar: 4.2g

Protein: 11.4g

Calories: 465

Calories from Fat: 166

Total Fat: 18.4g

Saturated Fat: 10.6g

Cholesterol: 143mg

Sodium: 214mg

Potassium: 670mg

Total Carbohydrates: 32.5g

Dietary Fiber: 7.1g

Sugar: 16.8g

Protein: 45.5g

11. Blueberry Shake
Preparing time: 5 minutes
Servings: 6

1. Ingredients:

250g blueberries
50g sour cream
80g oats
100ml coconut milk
160g pumpkin puree
Cinnamon, nutmeg for sprinkle on top

2. Preparation:

Mix all ingredients in a blender until the composition is smooth.

3. Nutritional facts (amount per 100g/entire composition):

Contains Vitamin A, C, iron, calcium.

Calories: 140
  Calories from Fat: 62

Total Fat: 6.9g
  Saturated Fat: 4.8g

Cholesterol: 4mg
Sodium: 9mg

Potassium: 192mg

Total Carbohydrates: 18.5g
  Dietary Fiber: 3.5g

Sugar: 5.7g

Protein: 3g

Calories: 641

Calories from Fat: 371

Total Fat: 41.2g

Saturated Fat: 29.1g

Cholesterol: 22mg

Sodium: 56mg

Potassium: 1150mg

Total Carbohydrates: 112g

Dietary Fiber: 21g

Sugar: 34.4g

Protein: 18.1g

12. Peanut Butter Shake
Preparing time: 5 minutes
Servings: 6

1. *Ingredients:*

300ml almond milk
50g peanut butter
50g mix nuts
6 egg whites
1 teaspoon butter extract (5g)

2. *Preparation:*

Mix all ingredients in a blender until the composition is smooth.

3. *Nutritional facts (amount per 100g/entire composition):*

Contains Vitamin C, iron, calcium.

Calories: 236
    Calories from Fat: 191

Sodium: 109mg

Potassium: 241mg

Total Fat: 21.3g
    Saturated Fat: 12.2g

Total Carbohydrates: 6.2g
    Dietary Fiber: 2g
    Sugar: 3.1g

Cholesterol: 0mg

Protein: 8.3g

Calories: 1415

    Calories from Fat: 1148

Total Fat: 127.6g

    Saturated Fat: 73.1g

Cholesterol: 0mg

Sodium: 656mg

Potassium: 1448mg

Total Carbohydrates: 37.2g
Dietary Fiber: 11.9g
Sugar: 18.5g
Protein: 50.2g

13. Peanut Butter & Banana Shake
Preparing time: 5 minutes
Servings: 7

1. Ingredients:

250ml almond milk
2 bananas
30g peanut butter
5 eggs
2 teaspoons honey (10g)
1 teaspoon vanilla extract (5g)

2. Preparation:

Mix all ingredients in a blender until the composition is smooth.

3. Nutritional facts (amount per 100g/entire composition):

Contains Vitamin A, C, iron, calcium.

Calories: 191
  Calories from Fat: 126

Total Fat: 14g
  Saturated Fat: 9.1g

Cholesterol: 117mg
Sodium: 70mg

Potassium: 288mg

Total Carbohydrates: 12.5g
  Dietary Fiber: 1.9g

Sugar: 7.7g

Protein: 6.2g

Calories: 1339

Calories from Fat: 884

Total Fat: 98.2g

Saturated Fat: 63.9g

Cholesterol: 818mg

Sodium: 487mg

Potassium: 2015mg

Total Carbohydrates: 87.6g

Dietary Fiber: 13.5g

Sugar: 53.9g

Protein: 43.6g

14. Peanut Butter & Chocolate Shake
Preparing time: 5 minutes
Servings: 3

1. Ingredients:

2 tablespoon cocoa powder (30g)
30g peanut butter
250ml almond milk
50g whey protein

2. Preparation:

Mix all ingredients in a blender until the composition is smooth.

3. Nutritional facts (amount per 100g/entire composition):

Contains Vitamin C, iron, calcium.

Calories: 326
Calories from Fat: 240

Total Fat: 26.6g
Saturated Fat: 19.7g

Cholesterol: 35mg
Sodium: 89mg

Potassium: 472mg

Total Carbohydrates: 10.6g
Dietary Fiber: 3.5g
Sugar: 4.3g
Protein: 17g
Calories: 977

Calories from Fat: 719

Total Fat: 79.9g

Saturated Fat: 59.1g

Cholesterol: 104mg

Sodium: 267mg

Potassium: 1415mg

Total Carbohydrates: 31.8g
Dietary Fiber: 10.6g
Sugar: 13g
Protein: 51g

15. Chocolate Shake

Preparing time: 5 minutes

Servings: 6

1. Ingredients:

3 tablespoon cocoa powder (45g)

250ml milk

120ml pumpkin puree

1 teaspoon vanilla extract (5g)

5 eggs

2. Preparation:

Mix all ingredients in a blender until the composition is smooth.

3. Nutritional facts (amount per 100g/entire composition):

Contains Vitamin A, C, iron, calcium

Calories: 89

Calories from Fat: 44

Total Fat: 4.9g

Saturated Fat: 1.9g

Cholesterol: 140mg

Sodium: 73mg

Potassium: 185mg

Total Carbohydrates: 5.6g

Dietary Fiber: 1.4g

Sugar: 3g
Protein: 6.7g
Calories: 534

Calories from Fat: 267

Total Fat: 29.6g

Saturated Fat: 11.4g

Cholesterol: 840mg

Sodium: 439mg

Potassium: 1112mg

Total Carbohydrates: 33.8g
Dietary Fiber: 8.4g
Sugar: 18.2g
Protein: 40.4g

16. Chocolate & Almond
Preparing time: 5 minutes
Servings: 5

1. *Ingredients:*

2 tablespoon chocolate pudding (30g)
50g almond (chopped)
300ml milk
40g whey protein
1 teaspoon amaretto syrup (5g)

2. *Preparation:*

Mix all ingredients in a blender until the composition is smooth.

3. *Nutritional facts (amount per 100g/entire composition):*

Contains Vitamin A, iron, calcium.

Calories: 131

Calories from Fat: 61

Total Fat: 6.8g

Saturated Fat: 1.4g

Cholesterol: 22mg

Sodium: 70mg

Potassium: 154mg

Total Carbohydrates: 9g

Dietary Fiber: 1.3g

Sugar: 3.5g

Protein: 9.9g

Calories: 656

Calories from Fat: 303

Total Fat: 33.7g

Saturated Fat: 6.9g

Cholesterol: 109mg

Sodium: 351mg

Potassium: 770mg

Total Carbohydrates: 45.2g

Dietary Fiber: 6.5g

Sugar: 17.2g

Protein: 49.3g

17. Caramel and Hazelnuts Shake

Preparing time: 5 minutes
Servings: 4

1. Ingredients:

50g hazelnuts (chopped)
1 teaspoon caramel syrup (5g)
1 teaspoon maple syrup (5g)
250ml almond milk
50g whey protein

2. Preparation:

Mix all ingredients in a blender until the composition is smooth.

3. Nutritional facts (amount per 100g/entire composition):

Contains Vitamin C, iron, calcium.

Calories: 307

Calories from Fat: 211

Total Fat: 23.4g

Saturated Fat: 14.3g

Cholesterol: 26mg

Sodium: 37mg

Potassium: 326mg

Total Carbohydrates: 15.5g

Dietary Fiber: 2.6g

Sugar: 11g

Protein: 12.2g

Calories: 1228

Calories from Fat: 844

Total Fat: 93.8g

Saturated Fat: 57.3g

Cholesterol: 104mg

Sodium: 148mg

Potassium: 1303mg

Total Carbohydrates: 61.8g

Dietary Fiber: 10.4g

Sugar: 44.1g

Protein: 49g

18. Plum Shake
Preparing time: 5 minutes
Servings: 8

1. Ingredients:

200g plum
50g raisin
200ml milk
4 eggs
100g quark
70g oats

2. Preparation:

Mix all ingredients in a blender until the composition is smooth.

3. Nutritional facts (amount per 100g/entire composition):

Contains Vitamin A, C, iron, calcium.

Calories: 122

Calories from Fat: 43

Total Fat: 4.7g

Saturated Fat: 1.8g

Cholesterol: 87mg

Sodium: 62mg

Potassium: 149mg

Total Carbohydrates:
14.7g
Dietary Fiber: 1.3g
Sugar: 7.2g
Protein: 6.2g
Calories: 975

Calories from Fat:
340

Total Fat: 37.8g

Saturated Fat:
14.3g

Cholesterol: 699mg

Sodium: 499mg

Potassium: 1190mg

Total Carbohydrates:
117g
Dietary Fiber:
10.7g
Sugar: 57.7g
Protein: 49.7g

19. Tropical Shake
Preparing time: 5 minutes
Servings: 5

1. Ingredients:

1 banana
150g pineapple
40g mango
200ml coconut milk
1 teaspoon honey (5g)
50g whey protein

2. Preparation:

Mix all ingredients in a blender until the composition is smooth.

3. Nutritional facts (amount per 100g/entire composition):

Contains Vitamin A, C, iron, calcium.

Calories: 178

Calories from Fat: 94

Total Fat: 10.4g

Saturated Fat: 8.9g

Cholesterol: 21mg

Sodium: 25mg

Potassium: 294mg

Total Carbohydrates:
15.3g
Dietary Fiber: 2.1g
Sugar: 9.9g
Protein: 8.5g
Calories: 889

Calories from Fat:
468

Total Fat: 52g

Saturated Fat:
44.6g

Cholesterol: 104mg

Sodium: 124mg

Potassium: 1468mg

Total Carbohydrates:
76.4g
Dietary Fiber:
10.3g
Sugar: 49.2g
Protein: 42.7g

20. Peach Shake
Preparing time: 5 minutes
Servings: 8

1. *Ingredients:*

6 peaches
300ml milk
140g mandarins
30g oats
4 eggs

2. *Preparation:*

Mix all ingredients in a blender until the composition is smooth.

3. *Nutritional facts (amount per 100g/entire composition):*

Contains Vitamin A, C, iron, calcium.

Calories: 70

Calories from Fat: 20

Total Fat: 2.3g

Saturated Fat: 0.3g

Cholesterol: 57mg

Sodium: 34mg

Potassium: 137mg

Total Carbohydrates: 9.5g
Dietary Fiber: 1g
Sugar: 7.2g
Protein: 3.5g
Calories: 839

Calories from Fat: 245

Total Fat: 27.3g

Saturated Fat: 9.7g

Cholesterol: 680mg

Sodium: 405mg

Potassium: 1639mg

Total Carbohydrates: 115g
    Dietary Fiber: 12.4g
    Sugar: 86.2g

OTHER TITLES BY JOSEPH CORREA

Tennis Serve Harder Training Program

This DVD will teach you how to serve 10-20 mph faster in a 3 month day by day program. The best serve training program in the market. Video includes a 3 month chart training program and a step by step manual. The DVD shows you how to do the exercises properly and the process you should follow in order to be successful with the program.

Joseph Correa is a professional tennis player and coach that has competed and taught all over the world in ITF and ATP tournaments for many years. Besides being a professional tennis player he has a USPTR professional coaching certification and ITF kids coaching certification.

The 33 Laws of Tennis

The 33 Laws of Tennis is book full of valuable tennis concepts to help you become a better and more prepared tennis player. This book was written by a professional tennis player and coach in the USA. It's a very useful book that will come in handy when you least expect it and will remind you of many little but important things before competing.

Tennis Footwork and Cardio by Joseph Correa

Joseph Correa is a professional tennis player and coach that has competed and taught all over the world in ITF and ATP tournaments for many years. Besides being a professional tennis player he has a USPTR professional coaching certification and ITF kids coaching certification.

Get in better shape and improve your mobility on and off the tennis court. Your foot work will improve drastically as well as strengthen your core and upper body. This is definitely worthwhile for a serious tennis player no matter what your level. You become faster, stronger, and more agile and on the court as well as seeing an increase in acceleration in your groundstrokes and serve. Created by a professional tennis player for others to advance in their game and win more matches.

BONUS CONTENT

In appreciation, I am including bonus content which will benefit you more than you can imagine. You can download the pdf versions of my "post-match evaluation worksheet" to help you improve your match results and my "5 uncommon tennis strategies" by going to:

www.coachcorrea.com/pmew.php

www.coachcorrea.com/5uts.php

These are two great tools that will help you to develop your game to the best that it can be.

Good luck in your matches and practice sessions!

Made in the USA
Monee, IL
15 September 2021